EASY ENTE

—— RECIPE

★ AROUND ★
THE WORLD

To Dawn,
Thank you for looking
after me.
Love Lily
x

Five years ago with the encouragement of my friends at the Woodford Wells tennis club, I put together a collection of recipes that are easy to prepare and very tasty. I had no idea that the book would turn out to be such an amazing success.

It seems there are no limits to the talents of the lovely ladies of Woodford and my fantastic friends and family. Not only do they produce fabulous recipes but it turns out they are terrific salespeople as well! Over the last five years we have sold over 3,200 copies of the first Easy Entertaining book raising over £32,000 for Leukaemia and Lymphoma Research. The charity has just changed its name to Bloodwise but the fantastic work it does continues and grows each year.

Many people have asked me to do a second book of recipes so here we are again. This time the theme is recipes from around the world as we all have our favourites from holidays abroad or dishes from friends from overseas. We have also included a section this time around for street food which typifies the kind of food we all love, quick to prepare and tasty. I hope you like the dishes I have chosen.

I am again indebted to the help of a few key people without whom this book would not have been possible. Tony our photographer has patiently

photographed (and tasted) the seemingly endless set of dishes I put before him with great skill. My thanks must also go to my dear friend Jenny, Tony's wife, for all her help and support with the book.

I have again been blessed to have the incredible artistic talents of my niece Caroline who has done all the graphic design work on the book. Thank you, you're amazing.

Huge thanks also go to David Wright of G R Wright & Sons Ltd, who again agreed to cover the costs of the printing of the book. Due to his terrific generosity we are able to ensure that every penny raised from the sales of the book go directly to the charity.

Finally, my thanks go to my family for their support, eating their way through the mountain of recipes sent to me! As ever the biggest problem is what to leave out, their love and patience has been invaluable. Many people have kindly asked after the health of Clive, my husband, who has Leukaemia, and I'm delighted to report that despite a few setbacks he continues in good health – clearly due to all this fabulous food!

Thank you for buying this book, I hope you find many recipes in here that you and your family enjoy.

Lesley.
x

Bloodwise
Beating blood cancer since 1960

Bloodwise, formerly Leukaemia & Lymphoma Research, is a leading UK charity dedicated to improving the lives of patients with all types of blood cancer, including leukaemia, lymphoma and myeloma. We recently discovered that our old name was not widely recognised, and did not convey the range of what we do to the public.

This is why we chose Bloodwise - it embraces all blood cancer patients and unites everything we do from our research and thought leadership to our patient support services and fundraising.

Every year we stop more people dying of blood cancer and our researchers are working to stop people developing blood cancer in the first place. We improve the lives of patients with blood cancers such as leukaemia, lymphoma and myeloma because we believe everyone should be able to live their life to the full. We've been working to beat blood cancer for over 50 years and we won't stop until we do.

We're so grateful to everyone involved in this fantastic cookbook. The success of the first book was incredible and meant so much to Bloodwise. We couldn't do the work we do without brilliant supporters, so thank you also for buying this book - enjoy cooking the delicious recipes!

RECIPE CONTRIBUTORS

CONTENTS

MAINS

DESSERTS

STARTERS

PAT'S FRENCH ONION SOUP

Pat Deere sadly passed away of Hodgkin's lymphoma on 21 January 2015, aged just 59. He left behind so many happy memories for his family and friends, it would have been wrong not to include his favourite dish. Pat was a wizard of wit, able to make everyone laugh with his jokes and stories. He is sadly missed by all whose lives he touched, and now I hope that through this recipe you too will be able to share just a small part of the legacy he has left behind.

INGREDIENTS

50g butter

1 tbsp olive oil

1kg onions, thinly sliced

1 tsp sugar

4 garlic cloves, thinly sliced

2 tbsp plain flour

250ml dry white wine

1.3 litres hot beef stock

4 slices of French bread

140g Gruyere, finely grated

METHOD

1 Fry the onions in the butter and oil for 10 minutes in a covered heavy pan.

2 Sprinkle on the sugar and cook for 20 minutes more, stirring frequently until caramelised. Add the garlic for the final few minutes.

3 Sprinkle in the flour and stir well. Increase the heat, gradually add the wine and then the hot stock, stirring well. Cover and simmer for 20 minutes.

4 To serve, toast the bread and top with the Gruyere cheese. Grill until melted and serve on top of the bowls of soup.

ORIGIN: USA PREPARATION TIME: 5 MINS COOKING TIME: 40 MINS SERVES: 4

ALAN'S MARMA-STUD CHICKEN

I came up with this recipe at university when having friends round to watch sports on the weekend. We usually took turns making our own food and I've always liked adding a bit of heat to my meals, which is why I took the usual honey mustard chicken flavour and threw in some chilli!

INGREDIENTS

- 12 chicken wings
- 2 tbsp orange marmalade
- 1 tbsp wholegrain mustard
- 2 tsp chilli flakes

METHOD

1 Preheat the oven to 200°C/ Fan 180°C/Gas mark 6.

2 Put the chicken in the oven on a baking tray for 20 minutes.

3 Mix the marmalade, mustard and chilli flakes in a bowl until it becomes a thick paste.

4 Take the chicken out of the oven and smother in half of the sauce. Put it back in the oven for a further 10 minutes.

5 Turn the chicken over and spoon over the remaining sauce and cook for a further 10 minutes or until the chicken is cooked.

ORIGIN: AUSTRIA   PREPARATION TIME: 15 MINS   COOKING TIME: 30 MINS   SERVES: 6

LESLEY'S KNOBLAUCHSUPPE

This recipe for garlic soup came from a recent trip to Vienna. Don't be put off by the garlicky title it really is full of flavour with a generous hint, rather than a full out attack, of garlic. It is very versatile so use any vegetables you prefer.

INGREDIENTS

200g mixed vegetables (1 carrot, 1 celery stick, 1 small leek, parsley), finely chopped

90g butter

1 litre beef stock

1 tsp ground ginger

1 tsp caraway

1 large onion, chopped

4 garlic cloves, crushed

30g flour

METHOD

1 Sauté the mixed vegetables in 30g of butter until tender.

2 Add the stock. Bring to the boil and simmer for 20 minutes.

3 Put the soup in a blender until smooth.

4 Sauté the onion and garlic in the remaining butter. Add the ginger and caraway. Stir in the flour to make a roux.

5 Reheat the soup and stir in the flour mixture. Season to taste.

6 Serve with croutons or a sprinkling of parsley.

13

ORIGIN: IRELAND   PREPARATION TIME: 15 MINS   COOKING TIME: 20 MINS   SERVES: 6

JENNY'S BLACK PUDDING SCALLOPS

One of my favourite recipes from South east Ireland, originally eaten in Kilmore Quay a small fishing village overlooking dramatic scenery of Ballyteige Bay. It was served with white pudding but the thin slices of the black looks more effective. They went down a treat with half of guinness!

INGREDIENTS

6 scallops

150g frozen petit pois

6 slices of black pudding

65g bacon lardons

1 shallot, finely chopped

10g butter

1 clove garlic, finely chopped

10 mint leaves

50ml chicken stock

1 tbsp grated parmesan

1 tbsp olive oil

Squeeze lemon juice

METHOD

1 Sweat the shallots and garlic in the butter for 5 minutes. Add the mint, peas, and chicken stock and simmer for 5 minutes. Add the grated parmesan and blend the mixture in a liquidiser or with the back of a spoon until smooth.

2 Meanwhile, fry the black pudding for about 5 minutes on each side until slightly crispy. Set aside and keep warm.

3 Fry the bacon until crispy and add to the pea mixture. Add the olive oil to any remaining bacon fat and cook the well-seasoned scallops for about 1 minute on each side until golden brown. Squeeze a little lemon juice over the scallops whilst cooking.

4 To serve layer the black pudding and pea puree and top with the scallops.

JULIA'S THAI CRAB TARTLETS

The recipe says make your own cheese pastry which is nice but I have also used ready made pastry and the tarts are just as good! Also it uses tinned crab so there is no scary fiddling with fresh crab. They are really very tasty and can be made and baked a day ahead and reheated in a hot oven. They also freeze well.

INGREDIENTS

175g plain flour

1 tsp English mustard powder

75g butter, cut into small pieces

50g parmesan cheese

1 egg, beaten

FILLING

225ml double cream

2 eggs, beaten

340g tinned white crab meat

2 red chillis, finely chopped

2cm fresh ginger, finely grated

8 spring onions, thinly sliced

METHOD

1 Preheat the oven to 220°C/ Fan 200°C/Gas mark 7.

2 To make the pastry, in a food processor whiz the flour, mustard and butter until it resembles breadcrumbs. Add the Parmesan and the egg and mix until it forms a dough. Roll out and cut the pastry into the desired number of pastry cases.

3 Whisk the eggs and cream and season well. Pour into the pastry cases.

4 Drain the crab well. In a bowl, mix the crab and the other filling ingredients and seasoning and divide equally between the pastry cases.

5 Bake for 15-25 minutes until the pastry is golden and the filling set.

JO'S CHICK PEA CURRY (CHHOLE) AND BHATURAS

Our beautiful friend Maggie, who unfortunately lost her battle with cancer earlier this year arranged an Indian cookery course the year before, after we were trying to think of fun days together with the girls. I will always remember the day with very fond memories of great food and great friends.

INGREDIENTS

2 tins of chickpeas, drained
1 onion, chopped
1 tin chopped tomatoes
2 tsp ginger, finely chopped
½ tsp turmeric
1 tsp chilli powder
1 tsp garam masala
1 tsp cumin seeds
1 tbsp vegetable oil
Fresh coriander, chopped
2 tsp tamarind paste
1 tsp dark brown sugar

THE BHATURAS
300g self-raising flour
1 tbsp melted butter or ghee
8 tbsp yoghurt
Fresh coriander, chopped
Vegetable oil for deep frying
Pinch of salt

METHOD

1 Fry the onion with the cumin seeds in the oil until golden brown. Add the ginger, turmeric and chilli powder, stir constantly to avoid sticking.

2 Add the tomatoes and chickpeas. Mix well and add a little more water if needed.

3 Finally, add the tamarind paste, sugar, garam masala and fresh coriander and adjust the seasoning to taste. It should taste sweet and sour. Serve with rice or bhaturas.

FOR THE BHATURAS
1 In a large bowl mix the flour, salt and melted butter or ghee and coriander. Add the yoghurt and mix into a soft dough. Knead for 2 or 3 minutes then wrap the dough in cling film and let it rest for about 30 minutes.

2 Divide the dough into 15 balls and roll each into 8cm discs.

3 Heat the oil in a wok and fry each disc individually. They should puff up like balloons. Fry on both sides. Then serve with Chhole curry.

ORIGIN: SWEDEN   PREPARATION TIME: 10 MINS   COOKING TIME: 0 MINS   SERVES: 16

SALLY'S SALMON ON RYE BREAD

I am always on the lookout for a new canapé. This one caught my eye and has become a firm favourite with my family. You can't go wrong with smoked salmon, the rye bread makes a change from blinis and the colours are a lovely contrast.

INGREDIENTS

2 slices of rye bread

50g cream cheese

1 packet of chives, finely chopped

125g smoked salmon

1 heaped tbsp crème fraiche

1 heaped tsp creamed horseradish

METHOD

1 Cut the salmon into slices and place them in a bowl and mix in the crème fraiche and horseradish.

2 Sprinkle ¾ of the chopped chives onto a plate.

3 Spread the rye bread with the cream cheese and gently press the cream cheese side into the chives.

4 Slice each piece of rye bread into 8 squares and top each one with a teaspoon of the salmon mix and sprinkle with the remaining chives.

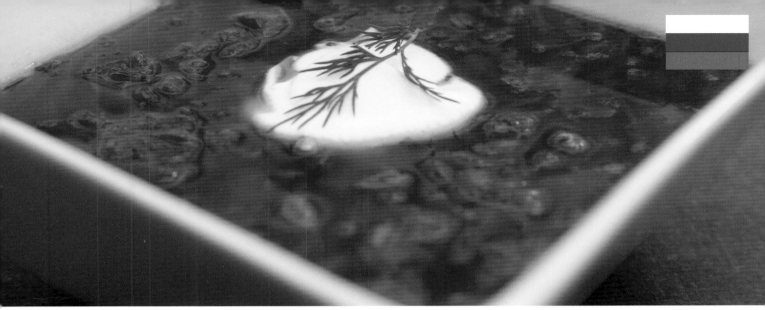

MARILYN'S BORSCHT

This recipe comes from an extraordinary Russian lady, Liudmila. In the 1970's food was so precious, it was lovingly prepared. In 1989 I was on a research trip to Chernobyl. From there I went to Kiev to visit Liudmila. In her small flat, she made this soup with its healthy ingredients from her stored vegetables.

INGREDIENTS

2 large raw beetroots, grated

1 small cabbage, finely chopped

1 red onion, finely chopped

2 carrots, cubed

2 potatoes, cubed

1½ litres of vegetable stock

1 tsp tomato puree

2 bay leaves

1 tbsp olive oil

3 garlic cloves, finely chopped

Juice of one lemon

Dill and soured cream to garnish

METHOD

1 Add the cabbage, carrots, onion, potatoes, tomato puree and bay leaves to the vegetable stock in a large pan. Simmer for 20 minutes.

2 Meanwhile, fry two of the cloves of garlic in the olive oil for a few seconds then add the grated beetroot. Fry for 10 minutes turning frequently.

3 Add the beetroot and the garlic to the stock. Stir in the lemon juice and season to taste, then simmer for 10 minutes.

4 Finally, add the remaining clove of garlic.

5 Pour into individual bowls and garnish with sour cream and dill.

19

ORIGIN: ITALY   PREPARATION TIME: 10 MINS   COOKING TIME: 15 MINS   SERVES:4

ALISON'S MOZZARELLA TART

I first discovered this recipe when hunting for something to use up the inevitable tomato glut at the end of the season. It has long become a family favourite as it is a real taste of summer. This recipe will make several individual tarts or one large one. The tarts can be round or square.

INGREDIENTS

375g ready rolled puff pastry
Jar of basil pesto
4-5 ripe tomatoes, thinly sliced
2 x 125g mozzarella balls, sliced
1 beaten egg
Basil leaves for garnish

METHOD

1 Preheat the oven to 220°C/ Fan 200°C/Gas mark 7.

2 Cut the pastry to the size of tart required. Score a line 1cm from the edge of the pastry and prick the inside with a fork.

3 Spread the pesto on the bottom of the pastry. Place the tomatoes and mozzarella, slightly over lapping, over the pastry.

4 Egg wash the edge of the pastry for a glossy finish and place in the oven for about 15 minutes until golden brown and bubbling.

5 Serve warm with scattered basil leaves on top.

ORIGIN: ITALY   PREPARATION TIME: 15 MINS   COOKING TIME: 15 MINS   SERVES: 2

CLIVE'S LIMONI COTTI AL FORNO

These stuffed lemons cooked in the oven are a perfect two bite starter. The recipe originates from the Amalfi coast and is very versatile. This version uses parma ham, mozzarella and tomatoes but you can use gorgonzola, pear and walnuts or substitute the ham for anchovies or olives, whatever you fancy.

INGREDIENTS

2 large lemons

1 or 2 balls of buffalo mozzarella cut into ½ cm slices

Fresh basil leaves

2 slices Parma ham

4 ripe cherry tomatoes, sliced

Olive oil

METHOD

1 Preheat the oven to 200°C/ Fan 180°C/Gas mark 6.

2 Remove ends of the lemons. Cut the lemons in half and carefully remove and discard the lemon flesh leaving 4 hollow lemon bowls.

3 Place a slice of mozzarella inside each lemon then build up layers of basil, ham and cherry tomatoes. Drizzle with olive oil and season.

4 Finally, top with another slice of mozzarella and bake in an ovenproof dish for 10-15 minutes until the cheese is bubbling.

5 Serve immediately with another sprig of basil and fresh bread.

21

JENNY'S SARDINIAN CULURGIONES

Ausilia and Monica are friends who live near us in Sardinia. They have taught me how to make culurgiones which are a very traditional type of pasta made only in some eastern regions of the beautiful island. Nonna's (grandmothers), mothers and children will make the pasta together, it is made using a simple flour and water recipe. Mangiare bene e godere (Eat well and enjoy). Nonna Jenny.

INGREDIENTS

PASTA
400g '00' or pasta flour
1 tsp salt

FILLING
250g mashed potatoes
100g pecorino cheese, grated
20ml olive oil
3 cloves garlic, crushed
2 tbsp mint or thyme, chopped

SAUCE
200ml passata
1 shallot, finely chopped
50g pecorino cheese, grated
Salt, pepper, sugar to taste

METHOD

1 Mix the flour and salt together in a mound slowly adding cold water. Mixing with your fingers until a dough forms. Knead until smooth and rest covered in clingfilm for 20 minutes.

2 Warm the oil with the garlic for 10 minutes. Mix the mashed potatoes, cheese and herbs and gradually add the garlic flavoured oil (not the garlic) until the mix is moist and creamy.

3 Roll out the dough until 3mm thick and cut out circles about 12cm diameter. Put a tablespoon of the potato mix in the centre of each and fold into a half moon shape and pinch carefully until fully sealed. Place in a large pan of boiling water, a few at a time, until they rise to the top and remove after about 5 minutes.

4 To make the sauce fry the shallot in the left over garlic oil, add the passata, cook down until thick, stir in the pecorino cheese and season with salt, pepper and a little sugar to taste. Pour over the pasta and serve.

SUZI'S CAMEMBERT IN BRIOCHE

Every bit of this dish is delicious, it is the ultimate savoury guilty pleasure. It can be served warm, but don't be tempted to cut it too soon! Slice it cold for a picnic treat.

INGREDIENTS

500g Wright's Brioche Mix
1 round of Camembert
8 slices Prosciutto
2 tbsp onion chutney
1 egg, beaten

METHOD

1 Follow the instructions on the pack to make up the brioche dough. Place in a bowl, cover with cling film and leave in the fridge for 30 minutes to allow the dough to stiffen.

2 Preheat the oven to 200°C/ Fan 180°C/Gas mark 6.

3 Roll out the dough into a circle of approximately 25cm. Lay the prosciutto slices on the dough.

4 Cover one side of the Camembert in chutney and place chutney side down on the prosciutto layer. Wrap the prosciutto around the camembert to cover it. Wrap the dough around the filling and turn over.

5 Brush with beaten egg and bake for approximately 20 minutes until golden brown. Serve warm but not too hot.

ORIGIN: ITALY   PREPARATION TIME: 10 MINS   COOKING TIME: 5 MINS   SERVES: 12

LESLEY'S PROSCIUTTO TOASTS

These tasty little canapés are so quick and easy to make. They are delicious on their own or served alongside a spring vegetable soup.

INGREDIENTS

1 ciabatta loaf, thickly sliced

Extra virgin olive oil

1 garlic clove, crushed

150g pack of soft goat's cheese

6 slices of prosciutto, halved

200g pesto

Small bunch of watercress

METHOD

1 Arrange the ciabatta slices on a baking tray and drizzle with a little olive oil.

2 Grill for 2-3 minutes each side until crisp and golden.

3 Rub the garlic over each piece of toast.

4 Spread each piece of toast with a little goat's cheese, a half slice of prosciutto, a teaspoon of pesto and a sprig of watercress.

5 Drizzle with a little olive oil before serving.

25

JANET'S MOULES MARINIERE

This dish is the one that immediately brings back the memory as a 14 year old on holiday feeling very grown up tasting mussels for the first time. It is still the best dish of mussels I have ever tasted served with hot salty bread and a very small glass of local rough red wine — however the glass of wine in my hand now is much larger when I make this dish. Cheers!

INGREDIENTS

1kg fresh mussels
2 tbsp olive oil
1 onion, finely chopped
2 garlic clove, finely chopped
150ml white wine
1 tbsp fresh thyme
150ml double cream
2 tbsp parsley, chopped

METHOD

1 Clean the mussels by scrubbing under running water, pulling off any beards and throwing away any mussels that do not close when you tap them.

2 Heat the olive oil in a heavy pan. Cook the onions and garlic until softened. Add the wine and when it starts to boil add the mussels and the thyme.

3 Turn the heat to low and steam the mussels with the lid on for about 4-5 minutes until the mussels open fully. Throw away any mussels that stay shut.

4 Add the double cream and cook for another minute. Scatter with parsley and serve with crusty bread.

ORIGIN: WALES   PREPARATION TIME: 20 MINS   COOKING TIME: 30 MINS   SERVES: 4

ROS'S ANGLESEY EGGS

I make this dish on every St. David's Day (March 1st) with Welsh Cakes as a dessert. It brings back childhood memories of my life in Wales. As a starter or a main dish it is perfect comfort food.

INGREDIENTS

2 hardboiled eggs

200g mashed potato

10g butter

1 leek, thinly sliced

25g cheddar cheese grated

100ml white sauce

METHOD

1 Preheat the oven to 200°C/ Fan 180°C/Gas mark 6.

2 Cook the leek in salted water for 10 minutes. Drain thoroughly and add to the hot mashed potato together with butter and seasoning, beat together thoroughly.

3 Spoon the mash into 4 oven proof ramekin dishes, top each with half a boiled egg.

4 Stir 2/3rds of the cheese into the hot white sauce and pour it over the eggs, then sprinkle over the remaining cheese.

5 Bake in the oven for about 20 minutes until the cheese is golden brown.

ORIGIN: ITALY   PREPARATION TIME: 20 MINS   COOKING TIME: 45 MINS   SERVES: 8

SCHIACCIATA

Schiacciata, simply means "squashed"! Variations of this Tuscan treat are made throughout Italy and the Tuscans mainly brush it with olive oil and sprinkle it with salt. It's all about the fabulous choice of fillings in this recipe. It will ensure a wow factor at any table.

INGREDIENTS

DOUGH
500g Wright's Ciabatta Bread mix
350ml water
2 tbsp olive oil

FILLING
6-8 slices Parma ham
400g antipasti
250g ricotta cheese

METHOD

1 Place the dough ingredients in a bowl and mix to a soft dough. Knead well for 5 minutes.

2 Divide the dough into 3 pieces and roll each piece out to about 20cm in diameter. Place each piece of dough in a well-greased deep round tin.

3 Scatter a third of the ham, antipasti and ricotta on top. Place another piece of the dough and another third of the filling on top, then repeat again with the final piece of dough and filling.

4 Cover with a damp tea towel and leave in a warm place for 40 minutes or until double in size.

5 Preheat the oven to 200°C/ Fan 180°C/Gas mark 6. Bake the Schiacciata for 40-50 minutes until well risen and golden brown.

ORIGIN: ITALY   PREPARATION TIME: 10 MINS   COOKING TIME: 10 MINS   SERVES: 4

JEAN'S PARMA HAM PARCELS

Years ago we went to a rather swanky restaurant while on holiday in Guernsey. I ordered "Parma Ham with Mozzarella and Honey" and these beautifully presented parcels arrived. I don't know how the restaurant did them, but I thought, let's give it a go, and found a way of making it without them falling apart!

INGREDIENTS

2 balls of buffalo mozzarella
8 slices Parma ham
Runny honey

METHOD

1 Preheat the oven to 180°C/ Fan 160°C/Gas mark 4.

2 Cut each Mozzarella ball into quarters.

3 Cut each parma ham slice in half, lengthways.

4 Wrap each cheese quarter in the ham to make a parcel.

5 Place on a lightly greased baking sheet and cook in the oven for 10 minutes until the cheese is bubbling.

6 Drizzle with a little runny honey and serve with a small side salad.

ORIGIN: FRANCE   PREPARATION TIME: 5 MINS   COOKING TIME: 0 MINS   SERVES: 4

LESLEY'S PEAR & ROQUEFORT SALAD

Roquefort is one of my favourite cheeses, rich strong and spicy. This dish takes minutes to make but tastes wonderful. You could add croutons or bacon lardons for variety or serve in small chicory leaves as a canapé. You can substitute any other leaves for the chicory if you prefer.

INGREDIENTS

50g Roquefort cheese

2 tbsp warm water

2 tbsp extra virgin olive oil

1 tbsp white wine vinegar

FOR SALAD

80g Roquefort cheese

Chicory, cut in ½ lengthways

100g walnuts, roughly chopped

1 pear, ripe but firm, finely sliced

1 celery stick, finely sliced

2 tsp chives finely chopped

METHOD

1 To prepare the dressing cream the 50g Roquefort in a bowl, add the warm water and stir until smooth.

2 Slowly whisk in the olive oil and vinegar and season with freshly ground pepper.

3 Mix the dressing with the chicory, walnut, pear, celery and 2/3 of the Roquefort.

4 Combine and arrange on a large serving plate or individual plates.

5 Finally crumble the remaining Roquefort over the salad and top with the chives.

31

CAROLINE'S BANG BANG CHICKEN

When I first started up my children's cookery school 3 years ago the theme was 'firework night'. Bang bang chicken spring rolls seemed to fit the bill perfectly. They are easy enough for 3yr olds to make and tasty for all palates. If you'd like more of the 'bang bang' then try adding more sweet chilli sauce to the dressing!

INGREDIENTS

1 chicken breast
3cm fresh ginger, chopped
½ carrot, grated
1/3 cucumber, cut into matchsticks
1 spring onion, thinly sliced
2 tsp toasted sesame seeds
4 sheets of filo pastry
A little sunflower oil

DRESSING
3 tbsp smooth peanut butter
1 tbsp sweet chilli sauce
Zest and juice ½ lime
½ tbsp soy sauce

METHOD

1 Preheat the oven to 220°C/ Fan 200°C/Gas mark 7.

2 Poach the chicken and ginger in water until cooked. Drain then shred the chicken into a bowl.

3 Put all the ingredients for the dressing in a pan and warm. Stir well then add to the chicken. Add the spring onion, carrot, cucumber and 1 tsp of the sesame seeds to the bowl and mix well.

4 Take 2 sheets of pastry and dab the first one with oil. Place the second on top and also dab with oil. Turn the pastry so that the corner is facing you.

5 Spoon half the filling in the corner then roll it over the filling folding in the outside corners towards the middle until you have a sausage shape.

6 Dab with more oil, sprinkle with the remaining sesame seeds and cook in the oven for 15-20 minutes until golden brown.

STREET FOOD

GERALDINE'S THAI CHICKEN SALAD

I first made this a few years ago for a girlie evening when everyone did one course. It's now become a firm favourite and I've passed on the recipe many times. If I can't get green papaya I just leave it out or use ripe papaya or cucumber or whatever I have to hand. The dressing is definitely the best part of this salad!

INGREDIENTS

2 chicken breasts
½ small white cabbage, shredded
1 large carrot, shredded
1 green papaya, skinned, deseeded and grated
Large bunch coriander, chopped
Bunch spring onions, chopped
50g peanuts, chopped

DRESSING
2 cloves garlic, finely chopped
3 bird's eye chilli, finely chopped
2 tbsp soy sauce
2 tbsp vinegar
2 tbsp sugar
1 tbsp lime juice
1 tbsp olive oil
½ tsp fish sauce
4 tbsp peanut butter
4 tbsp water

METHOD

1 Boil the chicken breasts and shred with two forks.

2 Mix together the chicken with the shredded vegetables in a large bowl and keep chilled.

3 Mix together the garlic, chilli, soy sauce, vinegar, sugar, lime juice, oil and fish sauce. Whisk until smooth.

4 Add the peanut butter and water and whisk again until creamy and smooth. Toss the salad with the dressing just before serving then add the peanuts.

ORIGIN: ITALY   PREPARATION TIME: 15 MINS   COOKING TIME: 30 MINS   SERVES: 6

PIZZA

Running the helpline at Wright's I have learned a great deal about why people like to make their own pizza at home with our Premium White bread mix. The 3 pizza's you can create from one packet can be dressed differently to cater for any allergens or dislikes within the family.

INGREDIENTS

500g Wright's Premium White bread mix

275ml warm water

50ml vegetable oil

1 onion, finely chopped

3 cloves garlic, finely chopped

1 tin of chopped tomatoes

Sliced chorizo

Jar of chargrilled peppers

Handful of olives

Mozzarella, sliced

Fresh basil

METHOD

1 Mix the water and oil with the bread mix to make a dough and divide into 3 balls. Roll out each ball and place on a baking tray. Cover with a damp tea towel and leave for 30 minutes until doubled in size.

2 Meanwhile, make the tomato sauce by gently frying the onion and garlic in olive oil, then adding the chopped tomatoes and season well.

3 Spread the tomato sauce on each pizza base and decorate with the chorizo, peppers, olives and mozzarella.

4 Bake in in a preheated oven at 220°C/Fan 200°C/Gas mark 7 for 15-18 minutes until golden brown. Scatter with the fresh basil.

ORIGIN: SPAIN   PREPARATION TIME: 10 MINS   COOKING TIME: 20 MINS   SERVES: 4

ROSE'S SPANISH TORTILLA

I used to watch a Spanish friend rustle up a tortilla for her children's tea. In my never ending quest to make healthier meals I sometimes vary this tortilla using sweet potatoes, butternut squash, celeriac and red onions adding some cubes of feta before finishing in the oven.

INGREDIENTS

1kg waxy potatoes, thinly sliced
1 onion, chopped
2 garlic cloves, chopped
4 eggs
Plenty of olive oil

METHOD

1 Fry the onions in 1 tablespoon of olive oil until soft. Add the potatoes, garlic and enough olive oil to cover the potatoes. Season well, put a lid on the frying pan until the potatoes are soft and the onions caramelised.

2 Pour the potato mixture into a colander to drain off the excess oil.

3 In a large bowl beat the eggs, season well then add the potatoes and mix gently.

4 Heat a tablespoon of olive oil to a frying pan and add the eggs and potato mixture until beginning to set. Then place the frying pan under a grill to "cook" the top of the tortilla. It is done when the egg is set.

39

ORIGIN: MEXICO   PREPARATION TIME: 10 MINS   COOKING TIME: 0 MINS   SERVES: 6

SOPHIE'S GUACAMOLE

I love the versatility of this recipe. It is perfect for large social gatherings served on crackers with prawns, or a night in on the sofa with a bag of Doritos. I would recommend using a blender and using ripe avocados, or your guacamole will resemble a mouldy couscous as mine did when I first made it.

INGREDIENTS

Handful of fresh coriander, roughly chopped

1 red chilli or pinch of chilli flakes

2 ripe avocados

1 garlic clove, crushed

5 ripe cherry tomatoes, halved

1 lime

METHOD

1 Scoop out the avocados into a bowl.

2 In a food processor blitz the coriander, tomatoes, avocados, garlic, chilli and the juice of the lime.

3 Season to taste. Serve with crudities, tortilla chips or rice cakes.

ORIGIN: FRANCE   PREPARATION TIME: 25 MINS   COOKING TIME: 15 MINS   SERVES: 16

CHEESE PESTO FOUGASSE

Fougasse is used to make the French version of calzone, which can have cheese and small strips of bacon inside the pocket made by folding over the bread. This takes its name from the Latin, panis focacius which was a flat bread baked in the ashes of the hearth.

INGREDIENTS

500g Wright's Ciabatta mix
350ml Water
100g Pesto
50g Pine nuts, toasted

TOPPING
50g Pine nuts, toasted
250g mozzarella cheese, grated

METHOD

1 Mix the bread mix with the water to form a soft dough. Knead well then cover with polythene and leave to rest for 5 minutes.

2 Add the pesto and 50g of pine nuts and mix, add more flour if required. Divide into 4 pieces and roll out into a rectangular shapes about 20cm x 25cm.

4 Make a large diagonal cut across the dough without cutting in two. Make 3 smaller cuts each side of the large cut and open out making a leaf shape. Repeat with the remaining pieces. Sprinkle with the toppings.

5 Cover with a damp tea towel and leave in a warm place for 40 minutes.

6 Bake in a preheated oven 200°C/Fan 180°C/Gas mark 6 for 15-18 minutes until well risen and golden.

LOTTIE'S MEATBALLS AND BUTTERBEANS WITH MANCHEGO

I'm never sure if I actually like the little terracotta tapas bowls more than their contents but there is something really exciting about a meal that consists of so many different dishes. I think the sign of a truly good tapas recipe is if you want to wipe the dish out with crusty bread so that the last bit of sauce doesn't go to waste.

INGREDIENTS

1 onion, finely chopped
2 cloves garlic, finely chopped
2 tbsp olive oil
1 carton of passata
16 ready-made meatballs
120g chorizo
1 tsp smoked paprika
Parsley, finely chopped
Small tin of butterbeans
Pinch dried chilli flakes
100g manchego, shaved

METHOD

FOR THE SAUCE
1 Sauté the onion and garlic in 1 tablespoon of olive oil until softened. Add the passata, bring to a simmer and season well.

FOR THE MEATBALLS
1 Fry the meatballs in the other tablespoon of olive oil until cooked and remove from the pan.

2 Fry the chorizo until the pan is red and oily, then add half the sauce, the meatballs and the paprika.

3 Heat through for a few minutes then serve in a tapas dish, sprinkled with parsley.

FOR THE BUTTERBEANS
1 Preheat the oven to 200°C/ Fan 180°C/Gas mark 6.

2 Mix the other half of the meatball sauce with the butterbeans, add the chilli flakes and half of the manchego.

3 Put in a tapas dish and top with the rest of the manchego. Bake in the oven until the cheese has melted.

ORIGIN: MEXICO   PREPARATION TIME: 15 MINS   COOKING TIME: 10 MINS   SERVES: 4

SUZI'S SPICY BEAN QUESADILLA

These are easy, quick and tasty. Quesadillas can be personalised to any pallet for anything you have in the fridge, adding left over chicken or chorizo works just as well as the beans.

INGREDIENTS

4 tortilla wraps

1 can of mixed beans in sauce

2 tsp chipotle paste

200g cheddar, grated

4 spring onions, thinly sliced

SALSA

1 small red onion, finely chopped

2 tomatoes, finely chopped

2 red chillis, finely chopped

Handful of coriander, chopped

METHOD

1 Make the salsa by mixing together all the ingredients, removing the seeds from the chillis for a milder salsa.

2 Mix the beans and the chipotle paste and heat in the microwave for 1 minute.

3 Heat a large frying pan and place one wrap in the pan. Spread over a quarter of the cheese and top with a quarter of the bean mixture.

4 Sprinkle the spring onions to one half of the wrap and fold over.

5 As the cheese starts to melt, and the wrap browns, carefully flip over to brown the other side. Carefully remove from the pan.

6 Cut in to two and repeat with the remaining wraps. Serve with the salsa.

MONICA'S APPLE MONTADITOS

Montaditos are a dish traditional from the north of Spain, especially the Basque Country. I first ate this dish at my friend Yam's place. It's simple but so delicious, everybody loves them and you can't go wrong. It's best served hot so just wait until the last minute to get them into the oven.

INGREDIENTS

1 french stick or baguette

2 goat's cheese logs, sliced

2 granny smith apples, peeled and thinly sliced

Runny honey

METHOD

1 Preheat the oven to 200°C/ Fan 180°C/Gas mark 6.

2 Cut the bread into 2.5cm slices and arrange them on a baking tray.

3 Put the apple slices on top of the bread and cover with a slice of goat's cheese.

4 Put a teaspoon of runny honey on each montaditos and heat in the oven for approximately 15 minutes until the cheese melts and goes brown. If necessary finish the cooking under the grill.

45

MIKE'S ISRAELI SHAKSHUKA

I make this spicy Middle Eastern dish as a quick delicious brunch. I first ate shakshuka in an Israeli beach cafe and it's perfect for a sunny summer morning or to warm you during the cold winter months.

INGREDIENTS

½ onion, diced

1 clove garlic, crushed

1 tbsp olive oil

250ml can cherry tomatoes

1 tsp cumin

1 tsp paprika

1 tsp cayenne pepper

2 eggs

Chopped parsley, to garnish

METHOD

1 Sauté the onion and garlic in a small cast iron skillet until softened.

2 Add the cherry tomatoes and the spices and season well. Simmer for 7-8 minutes.

3 Crack the eggs into the pan, cover and simmer until the eggs are cooked.

4 Garnish with parsley and serve with fresh bread, houmous and sour cream.

46

ORIGIN: MOROCCO   PREPARATION TIME: 10 MINS   COOKING TIME: 5-6 HRS   SERVES: 8

LOTTIE'S MOROCCAN LAMB WRAPS

This may be Moroccan in origin but my recipe is a tribute to the wrap stand in George Square, Edinburgh which appears during Festival season. It was such a welcome change to the normal festival fayre and every time I go back it is my first food stop after a busy morning of theatre going.

INGREDIENTS

½ lamb shoulder

1 Jar harissa paste

1 jar pasatta

1 onion, chopped

2 cloves of garlic, finely chopped

150g dried apricots, chopped

1 tbsp honey

100g flaked almonds

8 large wraps

Hummus

100ml Greek yoghurt

2 tbsp mint sauce

Pomegranate seeds

METHOD

1 Rub the lamb with half a jar of harissa and roast (170°C/Fan 150°C/Gas mark 3) on a rack in a roasting tray with a little water in the bottom of the pan for 5-6 hours. Top up the water if necessary and cook until the lamb falls away from the bone.

2 Fry the onion, and garlic until soft then add the pasatta, the rest of the harissa, apricots, honey and almonds until heated through.

When the lamb is cooked pull it apart and add to the sauce. Sprinkle with pomegranate seeds.

3 To make the yoghurt dressing add the mint sauce to the yoghurt and stir well.

4 To assemble the wraps, spread a wrap with hummus, add two tablespoons of lamb mixture and top with the yoghurt mix. Roll and eat.

47

ALISON'S ARMENIAN DOLMA

Made with the fresh vine leaves from Grandma Carapiet's garden, this recipe has been a family favourite for years. It is equally delicious with shop bought leaves or even cabbage leaves. The dolma is easy to make and the baharat, a traditional Armenian spice mix, brings a lovely flavour.

INGREDIENTS

225g mince

100g rice

1 tin chopped tomatoes

2 tbsp tomato purée

1 tbsp Baharat spice mixture

2 tsp paprika

20 vine leaves

Lemon juice

Olive oil

METHOD

1 Soak the rice for ½ hour.

2 Combine the mince with the drained rice and add the chopped tomatoes reserving some of the juice for later. Add the baharat, paprika and plenty of salt and pepper. Add one tablespoon of tomato puree and mix.

3 Roll the meat and rice mix into the vine leaves to make sausage like packages.

4 Drizzle some olive oil into a large deep pan and line the bottom with left over or torn vine leaves to prevent sticking. Layer the dolmas in the pan.

5 Mix together the remaining tablespoon of tomato puree with the left over tomato juice, a squeeze of lemon juice and a tin full of water and season well. Pour over the dolma.

6 Press a plate on the top of the pan to hold down the dolmas during cooking and simmer for an hour.

ORIGIN: VIETNAM   PREPARATION TIME: 10 MINS   COOKING TIME: 5 MINS   SERVES: VARIES

LOTTIE'S VIETNAMESE SPRING ROLLS

We had just spent a harrowing few days getting across the border from Cambodia to Vietnam. When we arrived we were greeted by our guide holding packets containing all the ingredients we needed to make these rolls in the minibus. To this day whenever I make them the flavour takes me back to this wonderful country.

INGREDIENTS

Rice paper spring roll wrappers
Thai basil, Mint and Coriander
Spring onions, sliced lengthways
Cooked King Prawns

DIPPING SAUCE
3 tbsp lime juice
2 tbsp sugar
200ml water
2 tbsp fish sauce
1 red chilli, finely chopped
1 clove of garlic, finely chopped
3 spring onions, finely chopped

METHOD

1 Dip a spring roll paper in hot water to make it soft.

2 Lay it out on a board then place a few herbs and spring onions in the centre of the paper.

3 Top with 3 or 4 prawns then fold in the sides of the wrapper and roll up into a spring roll. Repeat until all the ingredients are used.

4 To make the dipping sauce heat the lime juice, sugar and water until the sugar dissolves. Then add all the other sauce ingredients.

5 Taste and adjust the mixture until you get the balance you like.

ORIGIN: HONG KONG   PREPARATION TIME: 10 MINS   COOKING TIME: 10 MINS   SERVES: 2

GILL'S HONG KONG PORK

A popular dish in our house, this recipe is quick and easy to make and very tasty. It is based on the fast, high heat cooking of Hong Kong that we enjoyed whilst on a visit to our son.

INGREDIENTS

2 pork steaks, cut into thin strips
1 red pepper, sliced
1 tbsp oil
5 spring onions, chopped
1 tbsp sesame seeds

MARINADE
2 tbsp soy sauce
2 tbsp sweet chilli sauce
2 tbsp sherry
2 tbsp dark brown sugar
2 garlic cloves, crushed
1 tbsp grated ginger

METHOD

1 Mix all the marinade ingredients and season, add the pork and chill for at least an hour or overnight.

2 Heat the oil over a high heat, add the drained pork and cook for 4 minutes.

3 Add the peppers, onions, reserving a few onions, and cook for a further 2 minutes.

4 Add any remaining marinade juices and cook for a further minute.

5 Serve with rice and scatter with the remaining spring onions and the sesame seeds on top.

51

DEBBIE'S GAMBAS AL AJILLO

I love to visit my dear friends in Spain and enjoy the tapas, in particular gambas al ajillo which is quick, easy and full of garlic flavour. I love fresh crusty bread which is essential with this dish of prawns and a pinch of chilli flakes that gives the sauce a slight bite.

INGREDIENTS

25 large raw tiger prawns
4 cloves of garlic, minced
1 tsp paprika
1 tsp chilli flakes
60 ml cognac or dry sherry
125 ml virgin olive oil
3 tsp chopped fresh parsley
Squeeze of lemon

METHOD

1 Warm the olive oil over a medium heat in a sauté pan.

2 Add the garlic and chilli flakes and sauté for about a minute.

3 Raise the heat to high and add the prawns, lemon juice, cognac or sherry and the paprika.

4 Stir well, then cook until the prawns turn pink, about 3 minutes.

5 Remove from the heat and transfer to a serving dish with the garlicky sauce. Season well, sprinkle with parsley and serve with fresh bread.

ORIGIN: BRAZIL   PREPARATION TIME: 5 MINS   COOKING TIME: 2 MINS   SERVES: 3

LOTTIE'S RUMP STEAK MARINADE

This is a recipe that I learnt whilst staying on a homestead in the Pantanal in Brazil. The beef was cooked on a "churrasco" or makeshift barbecue, and served with seasoned cassava flour and washed down with an ice cold caipirinha.

INGREDIENTS

Large rump steak
Lemon thyme, oregano chopped
1 clove crushed garlic
30ml extra virgin olive oil
Juice of half a lemon

METHOD

1 Cook the steak on a hot griddle or frying pan for approximately 1 minutes each side. (This dish works best if the steak is cooked rare).

2 Whilst the steak is cooking make the marinade by combining the herbs, garlic, oil, lemon juice and plenty of freshly ground salt and pepper in a shallow dish.

3 When the steak is cooked, place in the marinade for about 5 minutes each side.

4 Remove the steak from the marinade, place on a board and slice thinly.

53

JENNY'S MAKI AND ISO SUSHI

What a lovely birthday treat from Lesley to me; to learn how to make sushi. We had a fun time rolling and eating the sushi, which are remarkably easy and look impressive as canapes or starters.

INGREDIENTS

400g sushi rice

75ml sushi rice vinegar

Half cucumber, sliced lengthways

Sliced avocado

Crabsticks, shredded

Sliced carrot

4 sheets of nori

1 tsp sesame seeds

1 tsp chilli powder

METHOD

1 To prepare the rice, wash thoroughly in several changes of water until the water is clear. Place the washed rice in a large lidded pan with 440ml of cold water bring to the boil then reduce the heat to low and cook for 20 minutes. Add the vinegar to the rice and continue stirring and the rice will dry as it cools.

2 To make Maki place a ½ nori sheet down on a bamboo mat wrapped in clingfilm. Spread 80g of rice on the sheet leaving a 1cm gap at the top of the nori. Sprinkle sesame seeds along the centre of the rice. Place the cucumber along the centre of the rice.

3 Lift the edge of the bamboo mat and roll upwards and forwards until you have touched the top 1cm gap of the nori. Trim off each end before cutting into six slices.

4 To make the ISO place a ½ nori sheet shiny side down on the bamboo mat and spread on 80g of rice as above. Sprinkle the chilli powder all over the rice. Flip over the nori so the rice is against the bamboo sheet. Place the avocado, crab and carrot along the centre of the nori and roll into a cyclinder shape as above. Trim off each end of the ISO and cut into six pieces.

ORIGIN: FRANCE PREPARATION TIME: 15 MINS COOKING TIME: 35 MINS SERVES: 4

MARIE-THERESE'S POTATO GRATIN

I am French and my husband is Irish. The potato is a staple of the Irish diet and my husband would not regard a meal as being complete without it! I found this challenging but persisted, thinking how can I blend the cheese so beloved by the French to create a tasty melange.

INGREDIENTS

900g potatoes, thinly sliced
450ml milk
Large pinch of grated nutmeg
1 garlic clove, cut in half
100g Emmenthal or Cheddar
15g butter

METHOD

1 Preheat the oven to 220°C/ Fan 200°C/gas mark 7. Put the potatoes in a saucepan with the milk, nutmeg and seasoning, and simmer until just tender.

2 Grease a shallow baking tin and rub the sides with the cut sides of the garlic.

3 Transfer the potato into the dish with 150ml of the milk.

4 Sprinkle with the cheese, dot with the butter and bake for 20 minutes or until the cheese melts and turns golden brown.

ORIGIN: GREECE   PREPARATION TIME: 10 MINS   COOKING TIME: 0 MINS   SERVES: 6

MARGARET'S GREEK SALAD

Salads are one of my favourite meals when in Greece as the ingredients are always so fresh! They also go really well with Barry's favourite meal 'lamb chops' well, we are Welsh!!

INGREDIENTS

3 firm tomatoes

1 fresh cucumber

1 red onion

1 red pepper

50g black olives

200g feta cheese

100ml extra virgin olive oil

3 tbsp red wine vinegar

Fresh oregano

METHOD

1 Cut the tomatoes and cucumber into irregular pieces.

2 Slice the onion and the red pepper into rings.

3 Place in a salad bowl, season well, then add the oregano and the olives.

4 Cut the feta cheese into chunks and add to the bowl.

5 Pour over the oil and vinegar and mix well.

57

MAINS

SARAH'S HUNGARIAN GOULASH

This is a dish that was a family favourite when I was growing up. A wonderful winter warmer served with fresh chunks of bread. I can remember smelling the rich spices as it slowly cooked, waiting for dinner to be ready. So much so that I took the recipe with me when I left home and have been cooking it ever since.

INGREDIENTS

2 tbsp sunflower oil

3 sliced onions

1kg stewing steak, cubed

1½ tbsp paprika

¼ tsp cayenne pepper

1½ tbsp seasoned flour

2 tins chopped tomatoes

2 tbsp tomato puree

3 crushed garlic cloves

1 tsp crushed caraway seeds

2 glasses red wine or stock

500g cubed potatoes

METHOD

1 Fry the onions in half the oil in a heavy based casserole dish, then set aside.

2 Brown the meat in the remaining oil then cover with the flour, paprika and cayenne pepper.

3 Return the onions to the dish, then add all the other ingredients and cook either on a low heat on the hob (or in a preheated oven 180°C/Fan 160°C/Gas mark 4) for approximately two hours or until the meat is tender.

ORIGIN: JERSEY   PREPARATION TIME: 20 MINS   COOKING TIME: 35 MINS   SERVES: 4

ALAN'S BOULEY BAY BAKE

Inspired by the picturesque shores of Jersey, I wanted to share this delicious dish as it evokes a real holiday feeling for me – and I hope you'll feel the same! Combining land and sea, with wonderfully fresh sole and waxy Jersey Royal new potatoes, it's an instant classic that's simple to cook.

INGREDIENTS

500g plaice or lemon sole fillets

800g Jersey Royal potatoes

1 tbsp olive oil

1 lemon

Fresh dill

250g cooked peeled prawns

150g cheddar, grated

200g Greek yoghurt

2 tsp mustard

300g asparagus

1 tsp baby capers

METHOD

1 Preheat the oven to 200°C/ Fan 180°C/Gas mark 6.

2 Boil the potatoes for 15 minutes, drain and leave in colander to dry. Cut into 1 cm rounds and place on a roasting tray. Drizzle with olive oil, zest of lemon and a few chopped sprigs of dill. Season well and lay the fish fillets on top then scatter the prawns on the fish.

3 Put half the cheese in a bowl with the mustard, more chopped dill, yoghurt and the juice of half of the lemon. Cut the asparagus with a potato peeler and add to the bowl. Spread over the fish and finish with the capers and the remaining cheese.

4 Bake for 20 minutes until golden brown. Garnish with dill or asparagus.

ORIGIN: FRANCE   PREPARATION TIME: 15 MINS   COOKING TIME: 30 MINS   SERVES: 4

WENDY'S MONKFISH PROVENCAL

Being someone that's renowned for spending the least amount of time in the kitchen as possible, this recipe ticks the boxes! Very easy and delicious — my kind of cooking!

INGREDIENTS

4 x 150g monkfish tail fillets

200g bacon lardons

2 tbsp olive oil

2 tbsp chopped parsley

1 onion, chopped

3 cloves garlic, crushed

400g chopped tomatoes

2 tbsp tomato paste

1 tsp fresh tarragon, chopped

1 tsp balsamic vinegar

1 tsp caster sugar

METHOD

1 Preheat the oven to 200°C/ Fan 180°C/Gas mark 6.

2 Gently fry the onion and garlic in 1 tablespoon of the olive oil. Add the tomatoes, tomato paste, tarragon, vinegar and sugar, season well and bring to the boil. Pour into an ovenproof dish.

3 Season the skinned monkfish then fry quickly on all sides in the remaining olive oil for 3-4 minutes until brown but not cooked through. Place the fish on top of the sauce and cook for about 15 minutes.

4 Meanwhile fry the bacon for 10 minutes until crispy.

5 Remove the dish from the oven and sprinkle with the bacon bits and parsley.

63

ORIGIN: TOBABGO   PREPARATION TIME: 15 MINS   COOKING TIME: 3 HRS   SERVES: 4

RUDI'S TOBAGO BEEF WITH MANGO

In Tobago we love to 'suck mango' by biting through the skin and sucking out the very ripe soft flesh, especially when it's picked straight from the tree! I always add a dash of pepper sauce for a true taste of the islands but it's not essential.

INGREDIENTS

500g lean braising steak, cubed
2 tbsp vegetable oil
2 large onions, thickly sliced
750ml beef stock
1 ripe mango, cubed
Pepper sauce to taste (optional)

MARINADE
2.5cm fresh ginger, finely chopped
2 cloves of garlic, crushed
Zest & juice of one lime
2 tbsp soy sauce

METHOD

1 Mix together the marinade ingredients, toss the beef in the marinade and leave to marinate overnight or at least 4 hours.

2 Drain the beef reserving the marinade. Sear the beef in hot oil in a large lidded pan. Remove the beef and keep warm.

3 Sauté the onions until soft but not browned. Return the meat to the pan, add the marinade and stock and simmer for 2-2 ½ hours until tender.

4 Add the mango and raise the heat until the juice is reduced to a sauce.

ORIGIN: IRAN   PREPARATION TIME: 15 MINS   COOKING TIME: 1 HRS   SERVES: 4

CHRISTINE'S IRANIAN LAMB TABRIZ

This is an old family favourite passed on to me by my mum. If you love lamb, you'll enjoy this dish. It's even tastier if made the day before as the flavour develops. So ideal for dinner parties if you need more time on the day to concentrate on other courses! Enjoy!

INGREDIENTS

500g lamb, cubed

50g butter

100g cashew nuts, chopped

1 apple, diced

1 large potato, diced

1 onion, chopped

50g sultanas

1 tbsp curry paste

1 tsp cumin seeds

1 tin coconut milk

Pinch of salt

METHOD

1 Lightly brown the lamb chunks in the butter then move to a casserole dish.

2 Gently fry the onions in the same pan, add the nuts, apple and potato and cook for about 5 minutes.

3 Blend in the curry paste, cumin, sultanas and salt, then add to the lamb with enough coconut milk to barely cover.

4 Cover and cook very slowly on a low hob, or in an oven, 160°C/Fan 140°C/Gas mark 2, for about 40 minutes.

5 Serve with rice and cucumber raita (cheat by mixing mint sauce into plain yoghurt).

ANGELA'S ALGERIAN SHEPHERD'S PIE

Exotic Algerian Shepherd's Pie – A freeze ahead crowd pleaser! I first had this dish whilst staying at my cousin's and it has been a firm favourite of mine ever since. Packed with exotic spices and easy to make, it goes down well for a relaxed supper with friends served with a crisp green herby salad.

INGREDIENTS

1 tbsp olive oil

2 onions, thinly sliced

900g lean minced lamb

2 cloves of garlic, chopped

3cm root ginger, finely chopped

2 tbsp each of ground coriander, cumin and paprika

2 tsp ground cinnamon

450ml vegetable stock

100g dried apricots, chopped

Juice of half a lemon

TOPPING

1 kg waxy potatoes, cubed

Large pinch of saffron

2 tbsp olive oil

1 clove of garlic, chopped

Handful of fresh coriander, roughly chopped

METHOD

1 Preheat the oven to 200°C/ Fan 180°C/Gas mark 6. Sauté the onions in the olive oil until soft. Add the lamb and fry until brown all over.

2 Add the garlic, ginger and spices and season well. Stir in the stock and simmer covered for 20 minutes.

3 Add the apricots and cook for a further 20 minutes. Add the lemon juice then spoon into an ovenproof dish.

4 Meanwhile, boil the potatoes with the saffron and salt until tender. Drain well, return to the pan then stir in the oil, garlic and coriander.

5 Arrange the potatoes over the meat and bake for 30 minutes until the potatoes are crisp and brown on top.

ORIGIN: THAILAND   PREPARATION TIME: 10 MINS   COOKING TIME: 25 MINS   SERVES: 4

DAVID'S CHICKEN THAI RED CURRY

This is my current favourite recipe! I have cooked this recipe so many times and it is so simple with such lovely flavours that it has become a firm favourite in our house. It is easy to adapt too, sometimes I add cashews and prawns to make a deluxe version!

INGREDIENTS

4 chicken breasts, chopped

1 tbsp sunflower oil

1 spring onion, chopped

2 tbsp red Thai curry paste

400ml coconut milk

250ml chicken stock

2 tsp fish sauce

350g sweet potato, cubed

1 tsp lime juice

METHOD

1 Fry the spring onion in the oil for a minute and then add the curry paste.

2 Whisk together the coconut milk, chicken stock and fish sauce, add to the pan and bring to the boil.

3 Add the sweet potato and the chicken and simmer for approximately 20 minutes until the potato is tender and the chicken cooked.

4 Just before serving add the lime juice and serve with plain white rice and chopped coriander.

ORIGIN: FRANCE   PREPARATION TIME: 20 MINS   COOKING TIME: 25 MINS   SERVES: 6

JO'S TARTIFLETTE

This tartiflette recipe is one I have used in the last few years after trips to the Savoie area on girls ski trips. When we all get together to reminisce tartiflette fits the bill perfectly and this recipe tastes just like it does on the mountain and is an easy to prepare school night supper for twelve ladies!

INGREDIENTS

1kg charlotte potatoes, peeled and thinly sliced

250g bacon lardons

2 shallots, thinly sliced

1 garlic clove, crushed

100ml white wine

200ml double cream

1 whole Reblochon cheese (about 450g), sliced

METHOD

1 Preheat the oven to 200°C/ Fan 180°C/Gas mark 6.

2 Cook the potatoes in salted boiling water for 5 minutes until tender. Drain and set aside to cool.

3 In a frying pan, fry the bacon, shallots and garlic for 5 minutes until golden brown. Deglaze the pan with white wine and cook until most of the liquid has evaporated.

4 Layer the potatoes and bacon mixture in an ovenproof dish. Pour over the cream and season well with freshly ground salt and pepper.

5 Layer the cheese on top and bake until golden brown and bubbling.

69

ORIGIN: INDIA   PREPARATION TIME: 10 MINS   COOKING TIME: 45 MINS   SERVES: 4

GERALDINE'S CURRIED LENTILS

This is so easy to make and great with a griddled chicken breast to make a more substantial meal. I often make it on a Sunday and keep in the fridge to take to work for lunch during the week. I like it cold on a bed of salad leaves, or you can heat it up in the microwave!

INGREDIENTS

1 onion, finely chopped

3cm fresh ginger, finely chopped

3 cloves of garlic, finely chopped

250g lentils

3 heaped teaspoons curry powder,

1 heaped teaspoon cumin

250ml chicken stock

½ tin chopped tomatoes

Juice of one lemon

250g spinach

1 tbsp olive oil

METHOD

1 Sauté the onions, ginger and garlic in olive oil in a large saucepan. Season with salt and pepper.

2 Add the lentils, and spices and stir.

3 Add the chicken stock, lemon juice and tomatoes. Stir and cook loosely covered until the lentils are tender (30-40 minutes)

4 Add the spinach during the last five minutes and serve with Indian bread or rice.

ORIGIN: ITALY   PREPARATION TIME: 15 MINS   COOKING TIME: 40 MINS   SERVES: 4-6

JULIA'S PARMESAN MEATBALLS

I love this recipe. It is so tasty and easy to make and you can prepare it the day before and cook it when you need to. I use Coriander pesto as I prefer it to Basil but you could try both and see which you prefer!

INGREDIENTS

450g raw lean minced beef
25g fresh breadcrumbs
2 garlic cloves, crushed
50g parmesan cheese, grated
1 egg yolk
3 tbsp green pesto
Grated zest and juice of 1 lemon

SAUCE
1 onion, roughly chopped
2 celery stalks, thinly sliced
1 garlic clove, crushed
500ml passata

METHOD

1 Preheat the oven to 180°C/ Fan 160°C/Gas mark 4.

2 To make the meatballs, put all the ingredients into a bowl, add seasoning and mix gently together with your hands.

3 Shape into 24 round balls and leave in the fridge.

4 To make the sauce, gently fry the onion and celery in a large pan until soft.

5 Stir in the garlic, passata and season.

6 Drop the meatballs into the sauce and coat well. Cover with a lid and transfer to the oven for 25 minutes.

7 Serve with parsley and parmesan shavings.

71

LESLEY'S PAELLA

I love this spectacular dish with its vibrant colours and interesting textures. They are many different recipes for paella but this is my favourite and so easy to make. It is the perfect dish for sharing with friends, just add a crisp salad and a glass of Rioja and you are all set for a great evening.

INGREDIENTS

2 tbsp olive oil

1 large onion, finely chopped

250g chicken thigh fillets, diced

2 cloves of garlic, finely chopped

Large pinch of saffron

½ tsp paprika

3 tomatoes, peeled and chopped

500g paella rice

300ml dry white wine

1 litre of fish stock

200g monkfish, cut into chunks

50g peas

250g mussels or clams in the shell

300g cooked prawns

½ jar of roasted pepper strips

Chopped parsley

1 lemon, cut into 8 wedges

METHOD

1 Sauté the onion in the olive oil until soft. Add the chicken to brown then stir in the garlic, saffron and paprika. After 2-3 minutes add the chopped tomatoes and simmer for 8-10 minutes until soft.

2 Stir in the rice then add the wine and reduce by half before adding all the fish stock. Simmer for about 15 minutes or until most of the stock has been absorbed.

3 Add the peas, monkfish, mussels, prawns and pepper strips. Cover with a lid and cook for about 5 minutes until the mussels open up and the monkfish is cooked through and opaque.

4 Sprinkle over the parsley, dot with lemon wedges, season and serve with a crisp salad.

ORIGIN: CZECH REPUBLIC   PREPARATION TIME: 15 MINS   COOKING TIME: 20 MINS   SERVES: 4

MIA'S SCHNITZEL & POTATO SALAD

This is my favourite recipe from home in the Czech Republic. A lot of people would eat this on a regular basis but this is also one of the Christmas special menus. Each family would have a slight variation of this recipe. I love it the way my Dad does the potato salad and I hope you enjoy it too.

INGREDIENTS

4 veal, pork or chicken cutlets

2 tbsp cooking oil

2 eggs, well beaten

Flour

Breadcrumbs

5 large potatoes

1 onion, finely chopped

Small tin of carrots, diced

Small tin of petit pois, drained

5 gherkins, diced

2 tbsp mayonnaise

1 tsp mustard

METHOD

1 Pound the meat to tenderise until it becomes large and thin and season well.

2 On separate plates place the flour, eggs and breadcrumbs.

3 Heat the oil in a large frying pan. Dip the meat into each plate in turn then fry until golden brown on each side (about 2 minutes each side).

4 To make the potato salad, boil the potatoes in their skins until cooked. When they have cooled down scrape off the skin and break into small pieces in a large bowl.

5 Add the other ingredients and gently mix. This salad improves the next day if you can wait that long!

ORIGIN: WALES   PREPARATION TIME: 15 MINS   COOKING TIME: 80 MINS   SERVES: 6

BARRY'S CAWL

Well it doesn't get any more Welsh than this. The only accompaniment it needs is a bunch of daffs and Delilah playing on your music system. Muynheuuch y buyd!

INGREDIENTS

Half shoulder of lamb, diced
1 onion, chopped
1 small swede, diced
3 medium parsnips, diced
5 carrots, diced
2 large potatoes, diced
3 leeks, sliced
1 tbsp fresh thyme leaves
3 Bay leaves
15 Peppercorns

METHOD

1 Place the lamb and the onions in a saucepan and cover with water. Bring to the boil and simmer for 40 minutes. Allow to cool then refrigerate overnight.

2 The following day skim off the white fat and add the swede, carrots, parsnips, thyme, bay leaves and peppercorns. Reheat and simmer for 20 minutes.

3 Add the potatoes and the leeks and cook for a further 20 minutes or until the vegetables are cooked.

4 Serve with crusty bread.

ORIGIN: FRANCE   PREPARATION TIME: 10 MINS   COOKING TIME: 30 MINS   SERVES: 4

MARIE-THERESE'S SALMON PARCEL

I wanted my salmon to lay on a nice "flavour bed" — and I was reminded how my grandmother and my mother who lived through two world wars in Verdun worked to achieve good flavour when times were hard. So here we go: leeks are a great bed for my salmon to lay on, with crème fraiche as a duvet...

INGREDIENTS

800g skinless salmon in one piece
250ml crème fraiche
3 small leeks, finely sliced
Fresh dill

METHOD

1 Preheat the oven to 190°C/ Fan 170°C/Gas mark 5.

2 Line a baking dish with enough baking parchment to wrap the fish into a parcel.

3 Boil the leeks for 5 minutes to soften, then carefully dry them. Place them in the centre of the baking parchment.

4 Lay the whole salmon on top of the leeks and spread the crème fraiche evenly along the salmon. Top with sprigs of dill. Season well with salt and pepper. Bring up the sides of the paper to make a large sealed package.

5 Bake in the oven for 25 minutes.

ORIGIN: TOBAGO   PREPARATION TIME: 20 MINS   COOKING TIME: 1 HR   SERVES: 6

KELVIN'S SPICY CARIBBEAN BEANS

My grandmother taught me to make this. Large packs of dried red beans were imported into Tobago and sold in the only shop in our village, Lambeau. Grandma would trade whatever she had grown with the shop's owner in exchange for rice and beans. He would then take what he had traded to Trinidad to exchange it for pitch—oil (for lamps) and flour.

INGREDIENTS

1 onion, chopped

6 garlic cloves, crushed

2-3 tsp fresh ginger, chopped

4 tomatoes, finely chopped

½ stick of celery, finely chopped

½ tsp chilli, finely chopped

2 vegetable stock cubes in 1 cup of boiling water

4 x 450g canned red kidney beans

1 bayleaf

2 tsp black pepper

½ tbsp Golden Ray margarine

METHOD

1 In a large pan combine the onion, ginger, tomatoes, celery and chilli. Cook on a very low heat for 10 minutes, stirring frequently. Add the vegetable stock before the mixture dries out.

2 Add the drained beans, bayleaf and black pepper to the vegetable mixture. Add salt to taste and Golden Ray margarine if available.

3 Cook on a low heat for 45 minutes to 1 hour, stirring occasionally, until nearly all the juice has been absorbed.

4 Serve with rice or jacket potato and sour cream.

ROSE'S MOROCCAN LAMB

This was the first Moroccan tagine I ever had — my sister made it for a family gathering many years ago and it has stood the test of time. It just melts in the mouth with rich sweet spices. A perfect accompaniment to this would be a simply cooked couscous or quinoa stirred through with plenty of chopped fresh mint and parsley, spring onions and pomegranate seeds.

INGREDIENTS

1.5kg lamb, cubed

1 heaped tsp cinnamon

1 heaped tsp cumin

1 heaped tsp ginger

1 heaped tsp coriander

1 tbsp olive oil

2 onions, finely chopped

4 garlic cloves, finely chopped

1 tin chopped tomatoes

150g dried apricots, halved

150g pitted prunes, halved

Grated rind and juice of 1 lemon

700ml hot lamb stock

4 tbsp fresh coriander, chopped

1-2 tsp harissa

METHOD

1 Preheat the oven to 180°C/ Fan 160°C/Gas mark 4.

2 Mix the spices with salt and pepper and rub into the lamb. Brown the meat in the olive oil in an ovenproof pot.

3 Stir in the onion and garlic and cook for 1-2 minutes. Stir in the apricots, prunes, tomatoes and stock and bring to the boil.

4 Cover and transfer to the oven for about 1½ hours to 2 hours until the meat is tender.

5 Stir in the lemon rind and juice and fresh coriander, check the seasoning and top with a little harissa. Serve with couscous or quinoa.

ORIGIN: GRENADA   PREPARATION TIME: 15 MINS   COOKING TIME: 35 MINS   SERVES: 4

JOYCE'S SPICE ISLAND CHICKEN

This recipe is a sure favourite of mine. It is quick and easy to prepare and full of unusual flavours. It is also a very healthy dish.

INGREDIENTS

4 chicken breasts, skinless
1 red pepper, finely sliced
2 spanish onions, finely chopped
6 plum tomatoes, skinned, diced
1 tbsp sunflower oil
1 green chilli, finely chopped
Zest and juice of a lime
2 garlic cloves, crushed
1 tsp ground cumin
1 tsp ground coriander
½ tsp ground cinnamon
1 tbsp cornflour
300ml pineapple juice

METHOD

1 Preheat the oven to 190°C/ Fan 170°C/Gas mark 5.

2 Season the chicken well with salt and pepper and place in an ovenproof dish.

3 Place the tomatoes, chilli, lime juice and zest, garlic, cumin and coriander in a bowl and combine well.

4 Soften the onion and red pepper in the oil over a medium heat then add to the bowl.

5 Dissolve the cornflour in a little of the pineapple juice, then mix with the remaining juice and pour over the vegetables and season well.

6 Pour over the chicken, cover and bake for 35 minutes.

ORIGIN: USA   PREPARATION TIME: 10 MINS   COOKING TIME: 1 HRS   SERVES: 4

JULIA'S NAPA VALLEY CHICKEN

This is a wonderful recipe, it literally take 10 minutes to make. I have served it at dinner parties and it has always been a great success and very well received. The only problem is that when friends want the recipe you have to confess the very little amount of effort that went into entertaining them!

INGREDIENTS

500g skinless chicken thighs and drumsticks

2 cloves garlic, crushed

1 tbsp dried oregano

125ml red wine vinegar

50g pitted green olives

100g pitted prunes, halved

20g capers (optional)

150g brown sugar

125ml white wine

6 bay leaves

Chopped parsley or coriander

METHOD

1 In a large bowl combine the chicken and the other ingredients. Season well, cover the bowl and marinate overnight.

2 Preheat the oven to 200°C/ Fan 180°C/Gas mark 4.

3 Arrange the chicken and the marinade in a single layer in a shallow baking dish and roast for about an hour, basting from time to time.

4 Sprinkle with the parsley or coriander before serving.

KATE'S NORWEGIAN SALMON

This Norwegian salmon dish has now become a Friday night favourite. Given that my husband always swore that he didn't like fish, this is a minor miracle! Personally I half—cook baked potatoes in the microwave and then finish them off with the fish in the oven for 20 minutes.

INGREDIENTS

2 salmon fillets
2 tbsp peppercorns
2 tbsp olive oil

METHOD

1 Preheat the oven to 180°C/ Fan 160°C/Gas mark 4.

2 Using a pestle and mortar smash the peppercorns, then put them on a plate.

3 Brush the olive oil on the salmon and invert the fish on the plate to pick up the crushed peppercorns.

4 Cook on a foil lined baking tray for about 20 minutes or until the fish is cooked.

ORIGIN: ITALY   PREPARATION TIME: 10 MINS   COOKING TIME: 30 MINS   SERVES: 4

QUENTIN'S SPAGHETTI NAPOLITANA

If you locked me up for the rest of my life and told me that I could only eat one dish, this would be it. It's simple to make, and tasty. It freezes well and you can add anything to it such as bacon, salami, olives, mushrooms, chilli, peppers, pesto, whatever takes your fancy.

INGREDIENTS

2 tbsp olive oil
2 onions, chopped
2 garlic cloves, crushed
2 x 400g chopped tomatoes
Fresh rosemary or basil
175ml white wine
2 tbsp cornflour
500g spaghetti
Grated parmesan

METHOD

1 Sauté the onions in the olive oil until golden. Then add the garlic for a minute.

2 Add the tomatoes, herbs, and wine and season well.

3 Mix the cornflour with a little more wine or water and stir in to thicken the sauce.

4 Allow the sauce to simmer for around 15 minutes.

5 When the sauce is ready add the spaghetti to a large pan of boiling water for the time stated on the packet (taste regularly so ensure it doesn't overcook).

6 Drain the pasta, pour hot water over to remove any starch, add the sauce and scatter on the grated parmesan.

ROSE'S CHICKEN DHANSAK

Having been to India on a few occasions and sampled real Indian food I became interested in cooking a curry from scratch using fresh ingredients, minimising the fat content and delivering on flavour. This recipe isn't exactly authentic but it does tick a lot of the boxes! If you like spicy – just add more chilli.

INGREDIENTS

3 tbsp vegetable oil

1kg boneless chicken thighs

3 onions, finely chopped

5cm fresh ginger, grated

8 garlic cloves, crushed

2 red peppers, chopped

2 red chillis, finely chopped

6 cardamom pods,
split and husks discarded

4 tbsp ground cumin

3 tbsp ground coriander

1 tbsp ground turmeric

2 tsp chilli powder

2 tins chopped tomatoes

200g red lentils

1 litre chicken stock

3 tbsp white wine vinegar

3 tbsp brown sugar

6 tbsp natural yoghurt

Fresh coriander to serve

METHOD

1 Preheat the oven to 190°C/
Fan 170°C/Gas mark 5.

2 Brown the chicken thighs
in 2 tablespoons of the
oil, then remove with
a slotted spoon.

3 In the remaining oil, gently
fry the onion until soft,
then add the ginger, garlic,
chilli and the other spices
to the pan.

4 Add the tomatoes, peppers,
stock, lentils, sugar and
vinegar to the pan, then
add the chicken.

5 Bring to the boil, cover and
place in the oven for 1 hour
or until tender.

6 Stir in the yoghurt and serve
topped with coriander and
basmati rice.

ORIGIN: GREECE   PREPARATION TIME: 10 MINS   COOKING TIME: 3 HRS   SERVES: 4

WENDY'S BAKED GREEK LAMB

Baked lamb. A family Sunday favourite. Very easy to do and fool proof!

INGREDIENTS

800g lamb neck fillet
2 lemons
4 cloves of garlic
Handful of fresh parsley

METHOD

1 Preheat the oven to 150°C/ Fan 130°C/Gas mark 2.

2 Cut the lamb into 2.5cm pieces and place on a large sheet of foil in a roasting tin.

3 Cut 3 of the garlic cloves into slithers and using a sharp knife insert the garlic into the lamb.

4 Grate the zest from the lemons, set aside. Squeeze the juice from the lemons over the lamb and season well. Fold up the foil into a parcel and cook for 3 hours.

5 Just before serving finely chop the remaining garlic and the parsley and mix with the lemon zest. Spoon over the lamb.

ORIGIN: THAILAND   PREPARATION TIME: 15 MINS   COOKING TIME: 30 MINS   SERVES: 4

JULIA'S THAI VEGETABLE CURRY

The first time I made this was for my vegetarian friend Di and it was so delicious that all the non-veggies had second helpings too! It is very easy to make, although chopping the butternut squash can be hard work, and it's as good the day afterwards. If you have any left!

INGREDIENTS

1 butternut squash, cubed

1 onion, chopped

1 clove of garlic, crushed

1 sachet coconut cream

300ml vegetable stock

200g mangetout peas

1 tbsp red Thai curry paste

1 tbsp chopped fresh coriander

2 tbsp vegetable oil

METHOD

1 Preheat the oven to 200°C/ Fan 180°C/Gas mark 6.

2 Roast the squash, lightly oiled for about 20 minutes on a roasting tray until soft.

3 Meanwhile in a large pan soften the onions and garlic in the rest of the oil. Then add the curry paste, squash, cream and stock and simmer for a few minutes.

4 Add the mangetout, season well and bring to the boil and cook for a further 2 minutes.

5 Serve scattered with chopped coriander and lots of naan bread.

ORIGIN: WEST INDIES   PREPARATION TIME: 10 MINS   COOKING TIME: 20 MINS   SERVES: 4

JANET'S MANGO CHICKEN

This is one of my favourite recipes. It is so moreish and very easy to make. I love mango and it reminds me of Caribbean holidays whenever I make it and eat it!

INGREDIENTS

600g chicken breast, cubed
40g butter
1 mango, diced
4 spring onions, sliced diagonally
1 lemon, rind grated and juiced
200ml chicken stock
75ml crème fraiche
Pepper, nutmeg & paprika
Coriander, chopped

METHOD

1 Heat ½ the butter in a wok. Add the chicken and seal. Remove the chicken and keep warm.

2 Add the remaining butter to the wok, add the mango, spring onion and lemon rind and stir fry for two minutes. Return the chicken to the wok and add the stock and lemon juice and bring to the boil.

3 Boil on a high heat for 5-10 minutes, until reduced and thickened.

4 Season to taste with pepper, paprika and nutmeg and stir in crème fraiche. Garnish with coriander and serve with rice.

ROS'S SPANISH CHICKEN

This reminds me of hot summer days in Majorca. Sitting outside a restaurant by the sea and watching the world go by. Here's cheers to you all with another glass of Sangria!

INGREDIENTS

500g chicken, diced

1 tbsp olive oil

1 large onion, chopped

225g chorizo, sliced

3 cloves garlic, crushed

1 red pepper, sliced

1 red chilli, chopped

1 tbsp tomato puree

1 tbsp thyme, chopped

150ml white wine

850ml chicken stock

400g long grain rice

METHOD

1 Brown the chicken in a large frying pan, then remove the pieces and keep warm.

2 Gently fry the onion until transparent. Add the garlic and chorizo and cook for two minutes. Add the red pepper, chilli and tomato puree and cook for one minute.

3 Return the chicken to the pan. Add the thyme, white wine and chicken stock, cover with a lid and simmer for 30 minutes.

4 Stir in the rice and cook over a low heat for a further 15 minutes or until the rice is cooked and has absorbed most of the cooking liquid.

5 Leave to rest for 10 minutes off the heat, season to taste.

SAM'S LEMON FISH TAGINE

Lightly spiced, summery food; close your eyes and think Mediterranean and eating on a sunlit terrace.

INGREDIENTS

4 cod fillets

4 garlic cloves, finely chopped

3 yellow peppers, sliced

200g butternut squash, peeled and cubed

6 ripe plum tomatoes, roughly chopped

100ml vegetable stock

2 tbsp preserved lemon

250g rice

Crème fraiche

MARINADE

2 tsp ground cumin

1 tsp smoked paprika

1 tsp ground coriander

4 tbsp lemon juice

2 garlic cloves

Small bunch of coriander

METHOD

1 Blend the marinade ingredients in a food processor until smooth, saving a little of the coriander for the garnish. Rub half of it over the cod and chill for 50 minutes.

2 Preheat the oven to 200°C/ Fan 180°C/Gas mark 6.

3 Put the squash, garlic, peppers and tomatoes in a dish with the remaining marinade and stock, then season well.

4 Cover and bake in the oven for 20 minutes until the squash is soft.

5 Place the cod on a tray and grill for about 10 minutes. Serve with boiled rice, preserved lemon, the roasted vegetables and a spoonful of crème fraiche. Finally garnish with coriander and serve.

DESSERTS

JEAN'S TIA MARIA MOUSSE

We spent a couple of nights at a fantastic restaurant with rooms and this was on the menu, it was so light and delicious I had to have it on both nights. I tried to recreate the mousse at home using standard recipes but they were so stodgy and rich they were very disappointing. I experimented on the family and eventually found a winning formula!

INGREDIENTS

4 large egg whites
200g dark chocolate, 70% cocoa
75ml whipping cream
4 tbsp Tia Maria

METHOD

1 Break the chocolate into small pieces and melt in a bowl over a saucepan of boiling water. Remove and allow to cool for 15 minutes.

2 Beat the egg whites into soft peaks.

3 Whip the cream into soft peaks.

4 Fold the egg whites into the chocolate with a metal spoon, keep in as much air as possible, then add the Tia Maria. Fold in the whipped cream.

5 Divide the mixture into 4 wine glasses or 8 ready made chocolate cases and allow to set in the fridge for at least an hour.

ORIGIN: ARMENIA PREPARATION TIME: 15 MINS COOKING TIME: 30 MINS SERVES: 16 CIGARS

ALISON'S CIGAR PAKHLAVA

This attractive alternative to traditional Baklava comes from Armenia and came to me via my in laws. You'll love the hint of mellow lemony flavour which offsets the sweetness and complements the cinnamon and cloves. It's truly delicious and the cigar shapes are perfect to serve alongside a cup of coffee.

INGREDIENTS

1 pack of filo pastry
220g walnuts/pistachios
125g melted butter
1 tbsp cinnamon
3 tbsp sugar
½ tsp ground cloves

SYRUP
235ml water
350g sugar
85g honey
Juice of ¼ lemon

METHOD

1 Preheat the oven to 180°C/ Fan 160°C/Gas mark4. Simmer the water, sugar and honey for 10 minutes to make the syrup. Add the lemon and simmer for a further 10 minutes, set aside.

2 In a food processor pulse the nuts, sugar, cinnamon and cloves until crumbly.

3 Cut the filo into four equal strips. Take two strips of pastry and brush with melted butter, sprinkle with a tablespoon of the filing and roll into a cigar shape. Place seam side down in a buttered baking tray. Repeat until all the pastry is used. Brush with melted butter and bake for 30 minutes until golden.

4 Pour the now cooled syrup over the cooked cigars and allow it to be absorbed. Sprinkle with the remaining nut mixture to serve.

ORIGIN: SCOTLAND   PREPARATION TIME: 15 MINS   COOKING TIME: 9 MINS   SERVES: 8

SAM'S CLOOTIE DUMPLING

A childhood favourite, usually a birthday treat. A real winter warmer (as is all the best Scottish food, all the year round!). It would include little trinkets wrapped in parchment paper, with a silver threepenny bit (showing my age) for the luckiest. Not for weight watchers!

INGREDIENTS

250g margarine

2 eggs, lightly beaten

1 tbsp of golden syrup

500g mixed dried fruit

75g sugar

250g self-raising flour

1 tsp ginger or mixed spice

1 tsp cinnamon

4 tbsp milk

METHOD

1 On a low heat melt the margarine with one cup of water. Allow to cool slightly. Slowly mix in the beaten eggs.

2 Add the syrup, dried fruits and sugar to the mixture.

3 Add the spices to the flour and sieve slowly into the pot adding the milk as you do so. Mix thoroughly.

4 Line the inside of a bowl completely with cling film, folding it over the top edges. Add the mixture to the bowl. Cover with a plate and cook on high for 9 minutes.

5 Allow to cool slightly before turning out and serving.

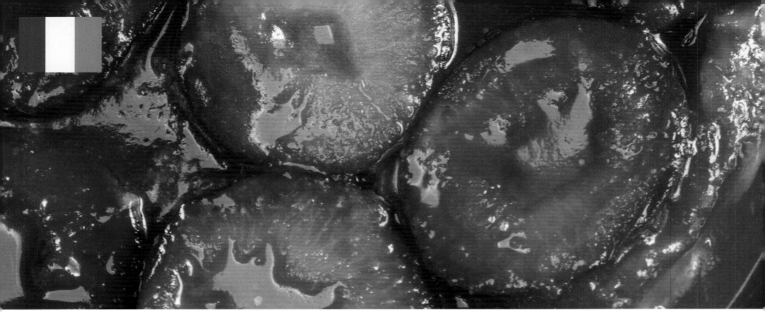

ORIGIN: FRANCE   PREPARATION TIME: 15 MINS   COOKING TIME: 30 MINS   SERVES: 6

MARGARET'S PLUM TARTE TATIN

This is a real cheat's version of tarte tatin. It is smart enough to serve at a dinner party and easy enough to make for a family meal. Try it with ripe pears or peaches served with cream, crème fraiche or ice cream. There will be none left for tomorrow.

INGREDIENTS

75g light brown sugar
6-7 plums, halved and stoned
100g marzipan, thinly rolled
1 sheet ready rolled puff pastry

METHOD

1 Preheat the oven to 220°C/ Fan 200°C/Gas mark 7.

2 Sprinkle the sugar in the base of a 23cm cake tin (not one with a removable base). Place the plums cut side down on top.

3 Cut the marzipan in to a round slightly smaller than the tin and place on top of the plums.

4 Cut the pastry slightly larger to cover the marzipan and tuck in the edges around the fruit. Make a small cross in the pastry to let out the steam then bake for 30 minutes until golden brown.

5 Carefully loosen the edges of the tart and invert onto a serving plate.

ORIGIN: THAILAND   PREPARATION TIME: 10 MINS   COOKING TIME: 30 MINS   SERVES: 4

LOTTIE'S MANGO AND STICKY RICE

Every street vendor and food court in Bangkok sells mango and sticky rice. The mangos are beautifully carved into hedgehogs, the art of which I don't think I will ever master, but this recipe still tastes amazing no matter how you cut your mango.

INGREDIENTS

100g sticky rice
400ml coconut milk
2 tbsp sugar
Pinch of salt
1 ripe mango, sliced

METHOD

1 Soak the sticky rice in a bowl of water overnight.

2 Drain the rice then wrap it in a muslin cloth and place in a steamer (or put in a sieve and place in a saucepan with a lid on) until it changes texture and becomes glutinous and sticky to touch.

3 Reserving a couple of tablespoons for later, warm through the coconut milk, with the sugar and a pinch of salt.

4 When the sugar is dissolved take off the heat and add the sticky rice and stir until the rice has absorbed the milk. Leave to cool.

5 Arrange the mango on a plate and serve with the rice, drizzled with the remaining coconut milk.

99

ORIGIN: SARDINIA   PREPARATION TIME: 10 MINS   COOKING TIME: 5 MINS   SERVES: 4

JENNY'S BOOZY SORBET

A variation of a Sardinian sorbetta which is served either frozen as a dessert or as a drink. Either way — Buono, especially when the sun's shining. If you want to cheat — just buy a lemon sorbet and add the booze!

INGREDIENTS

500g sugar
300ml prosecco
150ml limoncello
2 lemons, zest and juice
Few drops of lemon food colouring (optional)
Pinch salt

METHOD

1 Dissolve the sugar in 300ml water, stirring gently. Allow to cool to form a syrup.

2 Add the lemon juice, finely grated zest, salt, colouring, limoncello and prosecco and combine.

3 Pour into a plastic freezer box and freeze. After 2 hours give the mixture a stir. Gently turn every few hours to stop crystals forming, allow to set overnight and serve.

LORNA'S OSBORNE PUDDING

This pudding was a favourite of Queen Victoria and is named after her holiday home 'Osborne' on the Isle of Wight. She would frequently get her cook to make it when she visited. Although delicious this pudding is best recommended a little and not too often unless you want to resemble Queen Victoria in physique.

INGREDIENTS

50g unsalted butter

6-8 slices thick brown bread

2 tbsp marmalade

175ml whole milk

325ml double cream

1 vanilla pod

6 egg yolks

50g caster sugar

75g raisins

1 tbsp demerara sugar

Grated orange zest

METHOD

1 Preheat the oven to 170°C/ Fan 160°C/Gas mark 3. Grease a 23 x 18cm dish with butter. Spread the bread with butter and marmalade, cut off the crusts and slice diagonally.

2 Heat the milk, cream and the scraped out seeds and pod of the vanilla until just below boiling point. In a large bowl whisk the egg yolks and caster sugar then slowly add the milk.

3 Remove the vanilla pod. Pour a little of the mixture into the dish and add half the raisins. Arrange the bread in the dish with points upwards. Add the orange zest, rest of the raisins and the remaining milk mixture and stand for 30 minutes.

4 Sprinkle with demerara sugar and bake for 30 minutes. Leave to stand for 10 minutes before serving.

PAM'S TARTE NORMANDE

I learned how to make this tart from my sister while staying with her at their family cottage in the Charente-Maritime. She was given the recipe by an elderly French neighbour. It has become a firm family favourite. It can be made in advance and served either warm or cold. The almonds help retain moisture and add their distinctive flavour and texture.

INGREDIENTS

2 large cooking apples, peeled and thinly sliced

Shortcrust pastry tart

100g butter

100g sugar

2 eggs

50g flour, sifted

75g ground almonds

1 tsp vanilla extract

1 tbsp cinnamon sugar (or caster sugar)

METHOD

1 Preheat the oven to 190°C/ Fan 170°C/Gas mark 5.

2 Cream the butter and the sugar together thoroughly.

3 Stir in one egg at a time until thoroughly absorbed in the butter-sugar mixture.

4 Fold in the flour and almonds. Stir in the vanilla extract.

5 Spread the frangipane mixture evenly over the pastry case.

6 Lay the apple slices in overlapping layers over the frangipane and sprinkle with cinnamon sugar or caster sugar.

7 Bake for around 30 minutes until golden brown. Allow to cool on a wire rack.

ORIGIN: IRELAND   PREPARATION TIME: 5 MINS   COOKING TIME: 45 MINS   SERVES: 12

DEBBIE'S BAILEY'S TOFFEE TREAT

My friend loves Banoffee style desserts and this has a similar flavour which I often make for her – with or without bananas. The cake can be made 3 days ahead of when you need it so all you need to do is heat the Carnation Caramel as a sauce – quick, easy and delicious.

INGREDIENTS

500g Wright's Toffee Cake Mix
100ml Water
60ml Vegetable oil
100ml Bailey's
3 tbsp icing sugar
397g can of Carnation Caramel

METHOD

1 Preheat the oven to 180°C/ Fan 160°C/Gas mark 4.

2 Mix together the Toffee cake mix with the Bailey's, water and oil in a bowl to form a batter.

3 Pour this into a pre-lined or well-greased baking tray, approximately 27 x 17.5cm and bake for 40-45 minutes until springy to touch. Allow to cool.

4 Drizzle the cool cake with the icing sugar mixed with a few drops of water.

5 Warm the Carnation Caramel in a saucepan and serve with the cake. If you want the sauce a little thinner you can always add a couple of tablespoons of Bailey's to it.

ORIGIN: INDIA　　　　PREPARATION TIME: 15 MINS　　　　COOKING TIME: 30 MINS　　　　SERVES: 8

GEORGIE'S CARROT HALWA

I was introduced to this recipe by a friend and colleague, Neelima. It's a homemade Indian dessert made from carrot! I wasn't too convinced until I tasted it, and I have never forgotten it. It is lovely and sweet and goes really well with ice cream.

INGREDIENTS

200g grated carrot

2 tbsp ghee/clarified butter

180ml milk

2 cloves

3 tbsp condensed milk

2 tbsp sugar

½ tsp cardamom powder

Few raisins, almonds, cashew nuts lightly roasted in ghee

Few strands of saffron mixed in tbsp of milk

METHOD

1 Sauté the grated carrot for 8 minutes in the ghee on a low to medium flame.

2 Add the milk and cloves and allow to cook until the milk is almost absorbed. Add the sugar and cook for another 15 minutes. Add the condensed milk and go on stirring until it leaves the sides of the pan.

3 Remove the cloves, add the cardamom powder and saffron and mix.

4 Garnish with toasted almonds, raisins and cashew nuts.

105

ORIGIN: ITALY PREPARATION TIME: 10 MINS COOKING TIME: 15 MINS SERVES: 6

LESLEY'S VANILLA PANNA COTTA

We were shown this fool proof recipe when staying in a farmhouse cookery school in the remote mountain area of La Marche in Italy. Our wonderful teacher Jason describes the perfect panna cotta as having a wobble like a businessman's belly! Give it a go, it's so easy and tastes even better than it looks.

INGREDIENTS

3 sheets of gelatine
120ml milk
500ml double cream
60g caster sugar
1 vanilla pod split lengthwise

GANACHE
100g dark chocolate (minimum72%)
200ml double cream

METHOD

1 Soak the gelatine in a bowl of water. Heat the milk and remove from the heat.

2 Squeeze out the gelatine and stir into the milk pan.

3 Pour the cream into another pan, add the sugar and the vanilla pod and slowly bring to the boil stirring continuously. Remove the vanilla pod and stir the cream mixture into the milk mixture.

4 Rinse your molds, cups or glasses with ice cold water and shake out any excess. Fill with the mixture and refrigerate for 3 or 4 hours.

5 When ready to serve, make the sauce by melting the chocolate in a bowl over simmering water. When melted, slowly whisk in the cream. Drizzle over the top of the turned out panna cotta.

ORIGIN: TURKEY PREPARATION TIME: 5 MINS COOKING TIME: 20 MINS SERVES: 4

LOTTIE'S TURKISH BAKED FIGS

I love this recipe so much that the first thing I did when I moved house was plant a fig tree in the garden. I have since found out that it takes five years for a tree to produce fruit so I will still be relying on the supermarket for some time to come!

INGREDIENTS

4 ripe figs
Honey
Cinnamon

METHOD

1 Preheat the oven to 190°C/ Fan 170°C/Gas mark 5.

2 Cut the figs in half and arrange in a baking dish.

3 Drizzle each half with runny honey and sprinkle with cinnamon.

4 Bake for 20 minutes and serve with crème fraiche.

JO'S CIOCCOLATA IN TAZZA WITH BACI DI DAMA (LADIES KISSES)

I was given an Italian cookery course for my 40th birthday by a few friends. We had a wonderful morning of Sunday morning market shopping, followed by cooking, then the best bit… eating! We cooked this lovely recipe for dessert and it is one that I have repeated again and again as it is so easy.

INGREDIENTS

225ml milk
200g double cream
100g caster sugar
5 egg yolks
150g plain chocolate (min70%)

BACI DI DAMA
100g hazelnuts, chopped
100g ground almonds
65g caster sugar
165g plain flour
175g salted butter, softened
½ jar of Nutella chocolate spread

METHOD

1 Pour the milk, cream, sugar and egg yolks into a saucepan over a medium heat and bring to almost boiling point. The custard should start to thicken and coat the back of a wooden spoon (if you run your fingernail through it the line remains visible).

2 Remove from the heat, add the chocolate and whisk to melt.

3 Serve in small coffee cups and drink it or dip strawberries or biscuits in it. If left to cool the chocolate will set and can be eaten next day.

FOR THE BACI DI DAMA
1 Preheat the oven to 180°C/ Fan 160°C/ Gas mark 4.

2 Mix the hazelnuts, almonds, sugar and flour and then using your fingers rub in the softened butter.

3 Take small teaspoons of the mixture and roll into a ball between your hands.

4 Put on a greased tray and cook for about 10 minutes.

5 When cooled sandwich two biscuits together with the Nutella.

ORIGIN: USA   PREPARATION TIME: 15 MINS   COOKING TIME: 30 MINS   SERVES: 8

JO'S KEY LIME PIE

Key lime pie originates from Key West, Florida in the 1800's. Keys people of that day had no refrigeration but they did have cans of condensed milk. They also had eggs, from chickens or other birds whose nests they managed to rob. The fresh taste of the limes makes you believe you are sitting in the sunshine in the Keys.

INGREDIENTS

95g butter

175g digestive biscuits

50g Grape-Nuts breakfast cereal

Zest of 3 limes

Juice of 5 limes

3 egg yolks

400g condensed milk

Lime slices to decorate

METHOD

1 Preheat the oven to 180°C/ Fan 160°C/Gas mark 4. Melt the butter in a pan.

2 Crush the digestive biscuits in a polythene bag, add the grape nuts and mix into the melted butter.

3 Press the mixture into the base and sides of a loose based flan tin and bake for 10-12 minutes until golden.

4 Meanwhile whisk the egg yolks and lime zest until thickened. Add the condensed milk and whisk again. Then add the lime juice and whisk again.

5 Pour into the baked crust and return to the oven for 20 minutes until just set.

6 Leave to cool then decorate with the lime slices.

ORIGIN: SWITZERLAND   PREPARATION TIME: 5 MINS   COOKING TIME: 5 MINS   SERVES: 6

RUTH'S TOBLERONE TART

I regularly make this tart for special occasions or family dinners. No real excuse is necessary. It's good as a large tart or individual or even for petit fours. For those who don't eat nuts a Terry's chocolate orange or mint aero are also delicious alternatives.

INGREDIENTS

150g Toblerone

142ml double cream

20cm sweet shortcrust pastry case, or 24 individual cases

15g white chocolate or raspberries to decorate

METHOD

1 Melt the Toblerone in a bowl over a pan of simmering water stirring occasionally.

2 Remove the bowl from the heat and stir in the cream until thoroughly mixed.

3 Leave to cool for 10 minutes then pour into the pastry.

4 Chill in the fridge for two hours then decorate with grated white chocolate or raspberries.

CLAIRE'S SHRIKAND

This delicious dessert hails from Gujarat, northern India, my husband's Auntie gave me the recipe. Very simple to make. It works great as a special sweet treat after a spicy curry, and is often served at Indian weddings.

INGREDIENTS

500ml Greek Yoghurt
Milk for infusing
½ tsp saffron strands
6-8 tbsp icing sugar, to taste
¼ tsp freshly ground green cardamom seeds

GARNISH
2 tbsp chopped unsalted pistachio nuts
Pomegranate seeds
Edible silver leaf

METHOD

1 Line a sieve with a clean muslin cloth and place over a clean bowl.

2 Place the yoghurt in the muslin. Cover and place in the fridge, overnight to allow liquid to drain off.

3 When all the liquid has drained (you can squeeze the excess out by turning the muslin), discard the liquid and put the yoghurt in a bowl.

4 Heat a small amount of milk in a saucepan, put two teaspoons of the milk in a small bowl and crumble in the saffron. Leave to infuse for 10 minutes then crush the saffron into the milk with the back of a spoon.

5 Add the saffron milk, icing sugar and cardamom to the yoghurt and mix well. Cover and chill in the fridge. Garnish with the nuts, pomegranate or silver leaf.

RUM BABA

We used tinned peaches but a variety of fruits can be used, especially those suitable for being soaked in rum — yum yum! The modern baba au rhum (rum baba), with dried fruit and soaking in rum, was invented in Paris, in the 19th century.

INGREDIENTS

250g Wright's Ciabatta Bread Mix

1 tbsp caster sugar

50g butter, softened

3 eggs

85ml warm water

1 tsp vanilla essence

SYRUP

250g sugar

500ml boiling water

25ml rum

METHOD

1 Mix the dough ingredients together to make a smooth batter. Divide into 12 well-greased muffin tins.

2 Cover with a damp tea towel and leave in a warm place to prove for 40 minutes, then bake for 12-15 minutes until golden in a preheated oven 200°C/Fan 180°C/Gas mark 6.

3 Stand for 5 minutes before removing from the tins and leaving to cool on a wire tray. Whilst cooling, heat the syrup ingredients together. Soak each baba in the hot syrup and replace on the cooling tray.

4 When cool decorate with whipped cream and fruit.

ORIGIN: ITALY   PREPARATION TIME: 30 MINS   COOKING TIME: 0 MINS   SERVES: 6

IRENE'S TIRAMISU

The origins of this Italian dish date back to the infamous De Medici family and to the Grand Duke Cosimo De Medici, in particular. Apparently, he had his chef design this dish as an aphrodisiac for his new mistress. Whether or not it worked and whether this story is true I cannot tell!

INGREDIENTS

300ml double cream

300g mascarpone cheese

2 tbsp caster sugar

1 tsp vanilla extract

24 sponge fingers

1 cup of strong coffee

6 tbsp Tia Maria (use Amaretto, Baileys or rum if preferred)

1 tbsp of coca powder

METHOD

1 Make 1 cup of strong coffee (4 tsp instant coffee plus 1 tbsp sugar) and leave to cool.

2 Whip the cream and the caster sugar together.

3 Mix together the Tia Maria, mascarpone and vanilla extract, then gently fold into the cream mixture.

4 Dip half of the sponge fingers into the coffee and line a serving dish. Cover with half of the cream mixture.

5 Add a second layer of coffee soaked sponges and the second half of the cream mixture.

6 Decorate with the cocoa powder and refrigerate until firm (about 2-3 hours)

ORIGIN: TOBAGO   PREPARATION TIME: 30 MINS   COOKING TIME: 45 MINS   SERVES: 8

PENNY'S RUM AND RAISIN SQUARES

I often make these delectable squares for my Tobago Christmas celebrations as a take on the traditional English mince pie. They are delicious as a dessert with coconut or vanilla ice cream. They can also be made smaller and enjoyed with a cup of coffee.

INGREDIENTS

150g raisins
60ml dark or golden rum
150g plain flour
30g granulated sugar
100g butter
2 eggs
200g brown sugar
50g melted butter
1 tbsp vinegar
1 tsp vanilla essence
1 tsp plain flour

METHOD

1 Soak the raisins in the rum overnight. Preheat the oven to 180°C/Fan 160°C/ Gas mark 4.

2 Mix the 150g plain flour, granulated sugar and 100g butter until crumbly. Press evenly into a well-greased 23cm square pan. Bake for 10-15 minutes until golden.

3 Whisk the eggs and brown sugar until blended. Add the melted butter, vinegar, vanilla essence and 1 tsp of plain flour and stir well. Mix in the rum raisins including any remaining liquid.

4 Pour over the prepare base and bake for 30 minutes until set and golden.

5 Cool in the tin for a few minutes, then mark the squares. Remove the squares and cool on a rack.

115

WRIGHT'S STOLLEN

Stollen dates back to 1560 when the bakers of Dresden offered the rulers of Saxony a Christmas Stollen weighing 36 pounds each as a gift. The largest Stollen was baked in 2010 by Lidl; it was 72.1 meters long and was certified by the Guinness Book of World Records, at the train station of Haarlem, Netherlands.

INGREDIENTS

500g Wright's Premium White bread mix

120g butter, softened

50g sugar

1 egg

2 tsp each lemon, almond and vanilla essence

260ml warm water

300g mixed fruit

100g mixed peel

25g mixed nuts

225g marzipan

50g glace cherries, chopped

1 tbsp granulated sugar for glazing syrup

METHOD

1 Add together the bread mix, butter, sugar, egg, essences and water and mix for 5 minutes to make a soft dough. Leave to rest for 5 minutes then blend in the mixed fruit, peel and nuts. Divide the dough into 2 equal pieces, mould round and rest for 5 minutes.

2 Divide the marzipan into 2 pieces roll each into a sausage shape.

3 Roll each piece of dough into a 20cm disc. Place the marzipan slightly off centre and sprinkle each with the cherries. Slightly moisten the larger area of dough and fold the smaller side over the marzipan to completely cover, leaving a slight lip of moistened dough.

4 Cover with a damp tea towel and leave in a warm place for 40 minutes or until doubled in size.

5 Bake in a preheated oven (200°C/Fan 180°C/Gas mark 6) for 30-35 minutes until golden brown.

6 Glaze immediately with the granulated sugar dissolved in a little boiling water. When completely cool dredge heavily with icing sugar.

INDEX